MW00435717

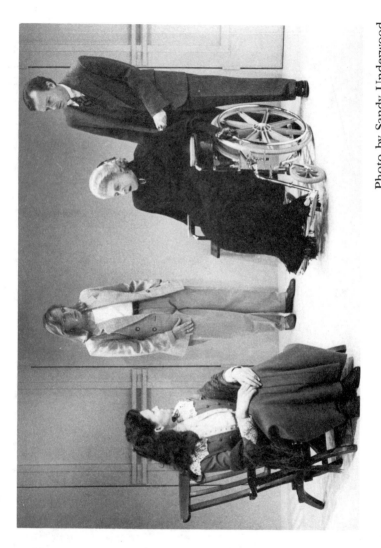

A scene from the Cincinnati Playhouse in the Park production of "Scotland Road."
Set design by Karen Teneyck.

SCOTLAND ROAD

BY JEFFREY HATCHER

★

DRAMATISTS
PLAY SERVICE
INC.

SCOTLAND ROAD
Copyright © 1996, Jeffrey Hatcher

All Rights Reserved

SPECIAL NOTE

SPECIAL NOTE ON SONGS AND RECORDINGS

For Lisa Stevens

SCOTLAND ROAD originally producd by Cincinnati Playhouse in the Park (Edward Stern, Producing Artistic Director; Buzz Ward, Executive Director), as the 1993 Winner of the Lois and Richard Rosenthal New Play Prize Winner, in Cincinnati, Ohio, in February, 1993. It was directed by Edward Stern; the set design was by Karen Teneyck; the costume design was by Delmar L. Rinehart, Jr.; the lighting design was by Kirk Bookman; the composer was Ronald Melrose and the stage manager was Bruce E. Coyle. The cast was as follows:

JOHN .... Reed Birney
HALBRECH .... Margo Skinner
THE WOMAN .... Lisa Fugard
FRANCES KITTLE .... Betty Low

SCOTLAND ROAD was originally presented as a staged reading at the 1992 National Playwrights Conference at the Eugene O'Neill Theater Center (Lloyd Richards, Artistic Director), in Waterford, Connecticut, in July, 1992. It was directed by William Partlan; the set design was by G.W. Mercier; the lighting design was by Spencer Mosse; the dramaturg was Tony Converse; the set renderer was Charles McClennahan and the production stage manager was Tom Aberger. The cast was as follows:

JOHN .... Reed Birney
HALBRECH .... Amy Wright
THE WOMAN .... Alice Haining
FRANCES KITTLE .... Helen Stenborg

CHARACTERS

JOHN — A man. Late thirties.

HALBRECH — A woman. Thirties, forties.

THE WOMAN — A woman. Late twenties, early thirties.

FRANCES KITTLE — An elderly woman. Eighties, nineties.

SETTING

A white room. Now.

AUTHOR'S NOTE

1) I had originally intended SCOTLAND ROAD to be a two-act play with an intermission placed after Scene 13. That's how it's usually performed, and that's how it's laid-out in this published version. However, a few recent productions have dispensed with the intermission altogether, and the result has been a taut, forward-moving 85–90 minute show. I'm completely comfortable with that option, liquor sales at the lobby bar notwithstanding.

2) The cast requirements are one man to play John, and three women to play the Woman, Halbrech and Miss Kittle. Why I stress this casting breakdown will be apparent after you've read the play.

3) MUSIC. Both "Nearer My God to Thee" and "Autumn" are hymns in the public domain. The music for "Autumn" is available in Episcopal hymn books. The music for "Nearer My God to Thee" is trickier. There are different versions of the melody. I recommend the one heard in the excellent British film *A Night to Remember*.* It's a more haunting tune than the bible-thumping version found in American hymnals. Besides, it's more in keeping with John's character that he sing a British version rather than an American one. Rent the video and listen for yourself.

* See Special Note on Songs and Recordings on copyright page.

SCOTLAND ROAD

ACT ONE

In the darkness:

A sound. Although not necessarily recognizable at first, it is the sound of a large, powerful ocean liner moving through the sea. The hum of the giant turbines, the low crash of waves as the prow cuts across the water.

The sound builds and builds. Then:

An image fades in: A blurred, black and white photograph fills the darkness. It is a photograph of a huge iceberg. An iceberg like a mountain, rising to a sharp pinnacle, surrounded by the black night.

It is a ghostly, wintry, frightening image. It fills the stage.

The sound of the ship driving through the waves builds. Holds. The image of the iceberg fades into darkness again.

The sound roars up, holds in the darkness for five more seconds.

Sound cuts off as the lights bump up.

Scene 1

A white room.

Stage right wall — a door, presumably leading to the out-side. Upstage wall — another door, leading to a bedroom.

High upstage center at the very top of the center wall is a small video camera peering down at the room, its red light glowing. White floor. An old-fashioned wooden deck chair is placed center. A very simple room. Very dry. Very still.

Halbrech and John stand in the room. Halbrech wears a white lab coat. She is in her 30s; sharp; wary; professional demeanor. John is in his late 30s. Very tightly wound, very brisk, alert, in-charge. A cool, wry, ironic "mid-Atlantic," al-most "British" demeanor. He speaks crisply, rapidly. He is effortlessly in command, never raising his voice.

Throughout the play, he wears the same tweed suit, impec-cably cut, of a style that would be fashionable in almost ev-ery decade of this century.

After a moment:

JOHN. Hotter.
HALBRECH. It's seventy-two degrees.
JOHN. Hotter. I want her to melt.
HALBRECH. This is *her* room. She is *my* patient. *I* am *her* doctor.
JOHN. Who's paying for it. *(Beat.)*
HALBRECH. Seventy-four. No hotter.
JOHN. I want this room kept completely clean. No books, no papers, no magazines. No one speaks to her. *(Points.)* Bed-room here. *(Points.)* Food brought in there. Your staff's con-tact: absolute minimum. Cameras are watching, microphones are listening. One of them whispers something to her, passes

8

a note, *anything* ... we'll see and we'll know and they're out.

HALBRECH.   They *can't* speak.

JOHN.   Maybe she doesn't either. One word muttered on board a fishing trawler does not a wordsmith make.

HALBRECH.   Your list arrived. *(Hands him paper.)* All the people she came in contact with since she was picked-up. Norwegian fishermen, Icelandic villagers, the doctor in Keflavik, his nurse.

JOHN.   *(Looking at list.)* Fourteen. None of them speaking English.

HALBRECH.   Keflavik is pretty isolated. The tabloid picked it up off the wire services via a Reuters stringer in Rekyavik. One of the crew phoned it in.

JOHN.   I read about it in the desert. The Badlands. South Dakota. 7:15 a.m. Gas station. Seven-11. Paying at the counter, looked down, saw the tabloid in the rack. I was here within 48 hours. *Your* report?

HALBRECH.   *(Consulting clipboard.)* Female. Caucasian. Age: 25 to 30 years. Height: five feet, four inches. Weight: 113 pounds. Hair: dark. Eyes: Blue. Green, sometimes. No physical damage. No surgical scars. No evidence of dental work — ever — in her life. Her clothes — dress, shawl, boots, stockings, petticoats, — all of makes, fabrics, fibers, dyes of approximately a century ago. *Possible* to duplicate today. Exposure to the elements. She was not wet. There was no salt water in her clothes. Dehydration and hypothermia suggest *some* time on the sea. *Days.* Not years.

JOHN.   Read the tabloid article. *(Looks off.)* One more time.

HALBRECH.   *(Reads from tabloid.)* "At 2:41 on the morning of April 15 of this year, a Norwegian fishing boat trawling 250 miles off the coast of Iceland spotted a small iceberg some three quarters of a mile to starboard. Sitting on the iceberg — dressed in a long, dark skirt and shawl — was a woman. When asked where she came from, she spoke only one word. The word was Titanic." *(Beat.)*

JOHN.   When does she come in.

HALBRECH.   Now. *(Blackout. End of scene.)*

Scene 2

Halbrech, John, and the Woman. She is as Halbrech described her, now wearing a white cotton robe and white slippers. Her hair is around her shoulders. She wears no make-up. She sits in the deck chair, her hands demurely folded in front of her on her lap.

HALBRECH.   This is the gentleman who brought you here. *(Pause. The Woman looks at John. He smiles at her.)*
JOHN.   I understand you're one of 99 women. Finnish. Swedish. German. Italian. Russian. Norwegian. Or subject of the United Kingdom. Are you glad to be out of those clothes? They've been cleaned. And examined. They're very nice. You're very lovely. You're a very lovely young woman. I understand you're over a hundred years old.

This will be your home. For a while. So much nicer than that village the boat took you. This is your sitting room. Food and drink provided. Attendants just on the outside of this door. The door *locks* whenever we go *outside* this door. Just press a button, and they'll come. Or *speak.* Speak and we'll hear you. Wherever you are. *See* you. Wherever you are. In this room. We want to help. You'll have to help us help you. *Speaking* will help.

You know Dr. Halbrech. Dr. Halbrech is the one who came to the village. Dr. Halbrech is the one who's been taking care of you. *Dr. Halbrech works for me.* I respect Dr. Halbrech's authority in all matters relating to your health, your comfort, and your well-being. But Dr. Halbrech works for *me.*

You'll be here indefinitely. We wish there were windows. But then you've seen so much of the outdoors these past 80 years.

You are apparently one of 99 women ... presumed "lost at sea" ... in a famous disaster. Finnish. Swedish. German. Italian. Russian. Norwegian. Or subject of the United Kingdom.

10

Dr. Halbrech will now repeat what I have just said in the preceding languages. *(Halbrech holds up her clipboard to read.)* HALBRECH. *(In Finnish.)* "Sina olet ilmeisesti yksi —" *(Blackout. End of scene.)*

Scene 3

Halbrech and John in the room.

JOHN. *(A small smile.)* Make it hotter.
HALBRECH. She's sleeping now.
JOHN. Make her soak the sheets with her sweat.
HALBRECH. She didn't speak on the trawler. She didn't speak in Keflavik.
JOHN. Crank it to a hundred and ten degrees. Fry an egg on her impassive brow.
HALBRECH. She will be kept in a proper climate and temperature. She will be properly fed and properly clothed. She will not be subjected to unwarranted anxiety. Even given these arrangements. And she will *not* be kept here indefinitely. No matter *what* you tell her. You *know* that. *Our agreement.* You have six days. *(Pause.)*
JOHN. *(Changing the subject.)* What evidence is there that she speaks at *all*?
HALBRECH. The report of the Norwegian fisherman.
JOHN. He could be part of the plot.
HALBRECH. Plot?
JOHN. *(Shrugs.)* P.R. Press. Publicity.
HALBRECH. For Norwegian fishing?
JOHN. We have to question the motives of everyone involved. Is there money to be made? A bestseller?
HALBRECH. *(Deadpan.)* "I DISCOVERED THE LAST SURVIVOR OF THE TITANIC"? *(Beat.)* By some Norwegian.
JOHN. Then the tabloid. Why didn't the tabloid do any follow-up?
HALBRECH. The same issue you saw in South Dakota carries a headline that reads "ALIEN MOTHER EATS BABY,

SELF." They're going to send *fact checkers* to Keflavik? Kaspar and Dane told me — *signed* to me — that she walked the bedroom floor before we brought her in. She doesn't like sitting in that deck chair.

JOHN.   It's authentic First Class.

HALBRECH.   They say she draws her hand across it as she passes.

JOHN.   *(Smiles.)* Nice touch. *(An idea.)* Dinner.

HALBRECH.   What?

JOHN.   *(Writing on a pad.)* Prepare ... this menu. Set the table ... *this* way. Let's give her something really first class. Nice and toasty. *(Pause.)*

HALBRECH.   Why do you want the temperature so high?

JOHN.   *(A small smile.)* Because I want her to say ... "air conditioner." *(Beat.)*

HALBRECH.   Six days.

JOHN.   You can cross the Atlantic in five. *(John hands Halbrech the pad. Blackout. End of scene.)*

Scene 4

John, Halbrech and the Woman. An elaborately laid out dinner — food, crystal, china, silver — is set on a silver tray on a wooden end table in front of the Woman.

JOHN.   That's quite a nice dinner you have. We thought the meals we'd provided you were rather on the skimpy side. This is more like it. More your sort of thing. *First Call for Dinner!* Go ahead. Don't mind me. *(The Woman looks at John. She looks at her dinner. She looks at John. Then she picks up a roll, breaks it, and nibbles off a small bite. To the Woman.)*

Let me tell you some interesting things. The *average* human being can survive without food or other solid material for approximately sixty-four and three-quarters days. The *average* human being can survive in the open cold for approximately seventeen days. The *average* human being can survive without water or other hydrates for approximately eight and a half days. *(Pause.)* I understand you floated on an iceberg in the North Atlantic without food, water, or shelter for *twenty-nine thousand two hundred fifteen days.* You're a remarkable young lady. "Young." Well. A gentleman would never bring up the subject. But perhaps I'm not a gentleman. Perhaps you're not a lady. Definitions have changed so for ladies and gentlemen. Maybe we can discuss just *how* those definitions have changed. Some day. Outside of here. Please go ahead. Eat. *(The Woman looks at John. She looks at her dinner. She looks at John. She picks up her water glass and drinks.)*

You'll note the gentlemen who attend you do not speak either. Unfortunately — unlike you — they *can*not. Speak. Since birth. They understand sign language though. I do not. They are, nonetheless, trained attendants. We don't discriminate against the deaf and dumb here. We're *supposed* to say "hearing impaired," but … *(Shrugs. Smiles.)* they can't hear us. I'm told you spend a lot of time every morning in the bathroom. The tub. The wash basin. I cannot tell you how difficult it was to obtain tooth powder. Well. Not *that* difficult. It's coming back, tooth powder. Modern conveniences don't have the richness and texture of the past. Something is lost in speed and ease. So they bring back tooth powder. Put it in a *tin*, sell it at six times the cost. Gives a pale, shallow soul the illusion of color and depth. Hell on the teeth, but…. Please. Don't mind me. Your dinner. *(The Woman looks at John. She looks at him a long time. She looks at her dinner. She looks back at him.)*

I understand you took a walk last night. Around and around these rooms. That's understandable. Your first night in new surroundings. New bed. New sounds. There's a hum in the wall, have you noticed, have you heard it? Like a motor. As if you're sleeping inside a huge machine, or inside a human being. Inside a ship at night.

You didn't flinch. That's good. Another "lady" might have flinched at the word "ship." A little flinch, a little twitch, a signal that deep inside your mind a recollection, a connection had been made. With the word … "ship." Thank you for avoiding such melodrama. But, of course, I forget: melodrama's not out-of-style yet where you come from. Perhaps you're even an actress? *(Pause.)* We have time. The world will wait. The world *has* waited. For eighty years.

Dr. Halbrech will now repeat everything I have said in Finnish, Swedish, German, Norwegian, Russian, and Italian. *(John signals to Halbrech. Halbrech holds up her clipboard, opens her mouth to speak. Blackout. End of scene.)*

Scene 5

Halbrech and John.

HALBRECH.   Your point?
JOHN.   The menu was the last dinner served in First Class that night. She didn't comment, of course, no "My, I just *had* roast squab the *other* evening." But she wouldn't use her forks.
HALBRECH.   Her *forks?*
JOHN.   Class question. We set a complicated formal silverware setting. First Class passenger would have known which fork to use when. Second Class, maybe. Steerage, highly doubtful. But she avoided using forks at all. And not a flicker of panic. And there's no greater panic than the panic in a faker's eye when the faker comes face to face with a full set of formal flatware and dowagers on either side.
HALBRECH.   Your *point.*
JOHN.   She's *good.* She doesn't want us to peg her easily. Either as … *(Indicates the list on Halbrech's clipboard.)* Mrs. H. J. Allison from First Class or … Miss Lena Solvang from Steerage. I'll want to see her alone tomorrow. But I'll need to find a new tack.
HALBRECH.   You haven't told her *where* she is. *(John looks at Halbrech. Blackout. End of scene.)*

Scene 6

John and the Woman.

JOHN.   This is America. Well. Not this *room*. Not for *you*. Not *quite*. Think of this room as "not quite America." That's where you were going, wasn't it? Or coming back to? This is new information. Before this, had you any idea where this room was? The village the fishing boat took you, that was not America, although I take it they were kind. But you've made it now. You've arrived. We're on the coast of the state of Maine. Very near the sea. Can you hear it? Listen. Close your eyes and listen. *(John closes his eyes. She looks at him.)* Are your eyes closed? *(John peeks open an eye. He looks at her looking at him impassively. He smiles a tight smile.)* I'm talking to myself, aren't I? *(John inhales, opens his eyes and changes gear.)* You had planned to arrive in New York on approximately April 17. Were you going to be met by someone? Family? Friends? A husband or fiancé? Children? Met by carriage or motorcar or private railroad? Maine is further north. A day's drive. Less. From New York. We could be in New York in less than a day. *(John smiles at her. Finally, the smile fades. Then: A deadly even tone.)* I could tear the sound out of you. I could *rip* it out. With my bare hands, with my nails, with my *teeth. (Exploding.) Make you...!* *(She looks at him. He stops. Beat. John snaps back to his clipped, cool demeanor.)* The preceding shall be repeated in Finnish, Swedish — *(Blackout. End of scene.)*

Scene 7

Halbrech and John. Halbrech glares at John. John looks away.

HALBRECH.   If it happens again —
JOHN.   It won't. *(Beat.)*
HALBRECH.   We're giving her the day off. *(John looks at*

Halbrech, his mouth opens to protest. She cuts him off.) After which you have twenty-four hours. *(Halbrech exits. John looks off. Blackout. End of scene.)*

Scene 8

Halbrech is sitting in the deck chair, reading a book. John enters from the outside. A beat.

JOHN.   *(Even.)* Where are Kaspar and Dane?
HALBRECH.   *(Still reading.)* Did you enjoy the day off?
JOHN.   *Where are Kaspar and Dane.*
HALBRECH.   Payday. They went into town. One of the video monitors went out. We'll need the repairman.
JOHN.   *(A slight catch.)* You, called someone?
HALBRECH.   *(Nods.)* You'll need to leave a check.
JOHN.   I'll leave cash. The locals prefer cash.
HALBRECH.   Did you enjoy your day off?
JOHN.   Day *lost.* What did *you* do?
HALBRECH.   Until now? Got up late. Took my bike along the coast road. Started a trashy novel. I checked the tabloids at the market. Nothing. Last week's shattering sensation — vanished beneath the waves. This week it's President Kennedy again. He was visiting his own grave at Arlington. "Exclusive photographs." Kennedy in a wheelchair. Jackie and Marilyn at his side. I don't know which is most improbable: Kennedy alive, Marilyn alive, or Jackie willing to be seen with them in public. Two weeks ago it was Jesus. At Kennedy's grave.
JOHN.   *(Has looked at watch.)* All right, let's begin.
HALBRECH.   *(Cool.)* You can start again in the morning.
JOHN.   Yesterday, at four-thirty p.m. you told me you were *ordering* a day off. It is now four twenty-seven p.m., twenty-three hours and fifty-seven minutes later. I can see her in three minutes.
HALBRECH.   *(Final.)* She gets the full day.

JOHN.   A "day" is twenty-four hour ...
HALBRECH.   *(Final.) She gets the full day. (Beat.)*
JOHN.   A "full day" is —
HALBRECH.   We have an agreement! I am her doctor! *Respect that! (Beat.)*
JOHN.   *(Miffed.)* It's cold in here. I think we should turn up the —
HALBRECH.   She leaves tomorrow. Sunday night. Eight o'clock. *(John turns his back to Halbrech.)*
JOHN.   She's trying to outwait me.
HALBRECH.   I don't think she's *trying* to do anything.
JOHN.   No? You think she's telling the truth? That she's not a fake?
HALBRECH.   There's a difference between not telling the truth and being a fake.
JOHN.   What a subtle and complex mind *you* have. But I forget: you lean towards the "innocent psychotic" scenario.
HALBRECH.   I'm a dispassionate scientist, I don't *lean.*
JOHN.   Then why are you here! For the sake of medical knowledge? For the gobs of money I'm paying you? For *kicks?*
HALBRECH.   *(Simply.)* She's my patient.
JOHN.   *(Dry.)* Yes. That too. You told me you would be "fascinated to have the chance to come back to America, to a *real* hospital and study the psychological make-up of a subject who, either (a) would devise an elaborate hoax in which she *pretended* to be a survivor of the Titanic; or (b) actually *believed* she *was* a survivor of the Titanic." Those *are* the only two possible reasons for your interest, correct?
HALBRECH.   No. There's a third reason. *(John smiles.)* The study of a man intent on destroying a woman. *(John's visage darkens.)* You want to prove she *isn't* something. How do you prove a negative? How do you describe an absence? *(Pause.)*
JOHN.   *(Stares off.)* You say nothing. I don't want to destroy her. I want her to tell me who she is.
HALBRECH.   *(Softens a bit.)* You haven't told her who *you* are. *(Blackout. End of scene.)*

Scene 9

John and the Woman. The Woman as before, seated.

JOHN. *(After a pause.)* Let's make a deal. You tell me something about *you* — and I'll tell you something about *me*. On April 10, 1912, the White Star Liner RMS Titanic departed Southampton, England, on its maiden voyage to New York. She was the largest, fastest, most glamorous ship in history. She was labeled unsinkable. *For* its maiden voyage, the Titanic carried on her the most glittering passenger list of the day. Names like Strauss, Harper, Hays, Dodge, Guggenheim, Rothschild. And ... others. On the evening of Sunday, April 14 at 11:40 P.M., the Titanic struck an iceberg at Latitude 41 degrees North, Longitude 50 degrees West, 400 miles off the coast of Newfoundland, tearing open five of its watertight compartments, and flooding the ship beyond repair. At 2:20 A.M., in the early morning hours of April 15, 1912, the Titanic sank beneath the waves of the Atlantic, carrying with it 1502 people.

My great grandfather died on the Titanic. My great grandfather was a gentleman. On the night of the disaster, he dressed his newly pregnant wife in a lifejacket, saw her safely to Lifeboat Number Four, kissed her, watched her lowered to the water below, and then returned to the Promenade Deck with his valet at his side and waited as the ship was dragged down to the bottom of the Atlantic. My name ... is the same as his. *(He kneels next to her.)*

This is a safe room. Clean. Dry. Clothes and food. *Warm.* You won't be punished, no matter what you say. Or don't. I'm not like that. No one here is like that. You think I want you to talk. I want to *listen. Difference.* There's a part of you I admire. The part that has been able to *do* all this. But the other part ... the "why" ... *(He gets very close to her. She turns to look into his eyes.)*

What if you whispered it to me? I wouldn't tell. I wouldn't tell a soul. It would be just you ... and me. There are some things you can't share with just *anyone.* But I'm someone you *could* share this with. I'm a kindred spirit. I understand. You see? I would try so *hard* to understand. *(Long pause as the Woman continues to stare at John. Finally, John, defeated, moves to the outside door, puts his hand on the knob.)* You leave tonight. *(Blackout. End of scene.)*

Scene 10

John is alone in the room, hovering over the end table. On it: an ice bucket, a bottle of champagne and three champagne flutes.

After a moment, Halbrech enters from the outside. She is not wearing her lab coat, instead she wears a raincoat and carries a briefcase and overnight bag. She closes the door behind her. Halbrech looks at her watch.

HALBRECH.   *(Wary.)* It's seven fifty-five. We're ready to go.
JOHN.   Last minute details. Kaspar and Dane been paid?
HALBRECH.   I gave them their envelopes. You gave them *cash.*
JOHN.   Better for them. Taxes.
HALBRECH.   We should be in Boston in three hours. The clinic's preparing a room. You've only got five minutes.
JOHN.   Agreed. Keys? *(Halbrech looks at John, then takes a key out of her pocket and drops it into John's hand.)*
HALBRECH.   *(Looks around room.)* Who'll handle the breakdown here?
JOHN.   *(Pockets the key.)* It'll be taken care of.
HALBRECH.   Will you be ... *sending* my check? *(John takes an envelope from his breast pocket, hands it to her.)*
JOHN.   Cash. Better for you. Taxes.
HALBRECH.   Thank you. Will you come to the clinic with us?
JOHN.   No.

HALBRECH.   In case she ... you know.

JOHN.   Well, if she "you knows" I'm sure I'll hear about it. *(Click. The bedroom door opens. Halbrech turns to look. The Woman enters. She is dressed in a turn of the century outfit. Long dress, puffed sleeves, lace, boots, shawl. Her hair is worn "up." She is wearing the outfit the trawler found her in.)*

HALBRECH.   *(Angry.)* I bought her an outfit to wear to the clinic, she can't —

JOHN.   *(To the Woman.)* You look lovely. Very much the way you want to be met when you leave this place.

HALBRECH.   *How did you get that dress!*

JOHN.   *(Deadpan.)* I learned some sign language on my day off. *(To woman.)* You're going to leave in a few moments. I would be less than truthful if I told you I *didn't* wish we had more time. But your doctor and I made an agreement, the details of which I should think you would want to know. *(John uncorks the champagne and pours three glasses as he tells his story.)*

When you were taken to the village of Keflavik, the good people there contacted a hospital in Rekyavik. Dr. Halbrech is a specialist in a certain area of study, and so she came to the village to take you back to the hospital *with* her. Fortunately, I was able to *intercept* Dr. Halbrech and offer her the chance of taking you to a much *better* hospital in America — a hospital in the city of Boston. *(John offers Halbrech a glass of champagne. She glares at him. He moves from her.)*

Dr. Halbrech was able to make the necessary arrangements. But before going to Boston, *I* wanted some time with you. Alone. Here. And Dr. Halbrech agreed to give me ... a *few* days. *(John offers the Woman a glass of champagne, but there is no response from her. He moves away.)*

But, in our case, that just wasn't enough. Still, I will look back on our time together fondly. I have held certain presuppositions in my mind: One, that you are a fraud. Two, that you may be part of a conspiracy. Three, that you want something you do not deserve. Four, that you pervert sacred memory. But I could be wrong. It's up to others now. The world you will find outside this door is much changed from the one you wish us to believe you left behind. You're on your own now. *(John toasts the Woman. He picks up the ice bucket and begins to sing "Nearer My God to Thee." Singing.)*

"Nearer my God to Thee,
Nearer to Thee.
E'en though it be a cross
That raiseth me;

Angels to beckon me
Nearer my God to Thee,
Nearer to Thee."

(Halbrech goes to the outer door, tries the knob. Nothing.) It's locked. *(Halbrech looks at John, moves to the video camera. It's red light is not glowing.)* It's off. *(Halbrech pounds on the door — three times.)* They're deaf you know. *(Halbrech whirls on John.)*

HALBRECH.   *Open this door!*

JOHN.   I have one more minute. *(John takes the key out of his pocket and dangles it in front of the Woman.)* After you. *(A long pause as John and the Woman stare at each other across the room. John's hand is outstretched towards the Woman. John walks towards the Woman, stopping a few feet away.)* Or don't you *want* to leave? *(John drops the key into the ice bucket and thrusts the bucket into the Woman's arms. Instinctively, the Woman grabs it, holding it against her. Halbrech turns on John.)*

HALBRECH.   What do you think you're doing! You think you can *buy* the right to do this, bring her to this place, interrogate her, frighten her, take whatever liberties you like, just because your name is *Astor!*

WOMAN.   *(Immediately.)* Astor. *(Halbrech and John turn to look at the Woman. The Woman looks back at them. As if it's a foreign word.)* As-tor. *(Then the Woman screams. <u>Screams</u>. The Woman collapses to the floor, the ice bucket falling out of her hands. Ice cubes splatter across the floor. Halbrech clutches the Woman, holds her as she shrieks on and on. Finally the screams stop. The Woman looks at the cubes on the floor. Whispers.)* Ice. *(John and Halbrech look at each other. Blackout. End of scene.)*

Scene 11

A few pieces of ice remain on the floor.

John is picking up the pieces of ice and plunking them into the ice bucket.

Halbrech enters from the bedroom and closes the door behind her. She holds her clipboard.

John keeps "plunking" the ice as she speaks.

HALBRECH.   *(Even tone.)* After the word "ice," she said the following: *(Plunk.)* "It's cold, it's cold, it's so, so very cold." *(Plunk.)* "Please don't make me go in the water. Please, please don't let the water come." *(Plunk.)* "Take me up. Take me up. Take me all the way to the Hebrides." "There are others." *(Pause.)* You have six more days. *(Halbrech turns and goes back into the bedroom. John examines a small piece of ice for a moment — then drops it into the bucket. Plunk. Blackout. End of scene.)*

Scene 12

John and Halbrech. Halbrech is handling a mountain of books, magazines, and papers.

HALBRECH.   *A Night to Remember* by Walter Lord; *The Loss of the SS Titanic; The Truth About the Titanic; The Discovery of the Titanic; Raise the Titanic; Look, the Titanic!; (Takes out a small white t-shirt.)* "I FOUND THE TITANIC AND ALL I GOT WAS THIS LOUSY T-SHIRT." You carry all this *with* you?
JOHN.   We're old friends. I can tell you on what line on which page every sentence lies.

HALBRECH. *(A slight smile.)* In Finnish, in Swedish, in German ...

JOHN. Know the material, but don't ever interrogate her by yourself. Leave that to me. You keep her healthy, I'll keep her wise. You call the clinic?

HALBRECH. *(Sheepishly.)* Told them the patient has a chill.

JOHN. *(Smiles.)* Have to raise the temperature.

HALBRECH. I want to warn you. We can't be sure she'll speak again. Last night was caused by a traumatic event. We don't know why she responded to your name, to the name "Astor," and we've let her go thirteen hours since. You could have full retreat. The rest could be silence. *(Blackout. End of scene.)*

Scene 13

John, Halbrech, and the Woman, dressed in her white robe and slippers again. The Woman looks out front.

WOMAN. My name is Winifred Coutts. I was born February 16, 1886 in Llechryd, Wales, Cardiganshire. My father was Gilbert Edward Coutts, a gardener. My mother Elizabeth Rhys-Mogg. My father died of convulsions from eating a cherry stone on October 29, 1904; my mother died six years later. In December, 1911, my aunt Mrs. Clara James procured for me a position in America in service as a parlor maid in the household of Mrs. George Haverland Coe of Pittsburgh, Pennsylvania.

On April 8, 1912, I set off by rail to Southampton where I arrived that evening and stayed in the Young Ladies' Hotel of Mrs. Edwina Flossie and her son Gerald until boarding the R.M.S. Titanic with a third class ticket, one chest, two carpet bags, one hat, one umbrella, two pair of shoes, two pair of gloves, two shawls, two dresses, three petticoats, one woolen coat, one hairbrush ... made of Dutch whalebone and real Spanish horsehair ... a copy of "The Strand Magazine," and one Welsh Methodist Bible belonging to my mother Elizabeth Rhys-Mogg Coutts who died of the influenza. I knew no one on board the Titanic. I had never been at sea before. On Sunday, April 14, I attended the services aboard ship at 10:00 A.M. in the morning and passed the rest of the day with others of my station. At 9:30 P.M. in the evening I retired to my bed. I read the Bible. Then fell asleep. A few hours later I was awakened by a sound. I don't remember anything after that. *(Pause. The Woman looks at John and Halbrech.)* I didn't appreciate the bit with the forks. *(She looks back out front. Blackout.)*

END OF ACT ONE

ACT TWO

Scene 1

Halbrech and John are alone.

JOHN. *(Deadpan.)* Yes, you're right, the rest might be silence.
HALBRECH. She's come out of her shell.
JOHN. We ran out of *tape.*
HALBRECH. She's said nothing that contradicts the basic facts known about the Titanic contained in this material. Everything checks out.
JOHN. But none of this material is classified. Anyone can dig it up in a library. Furthermore, if she tells us anything that does *not* appear in this material, it does not necessarily disprove her story be —
HALBRECH. — because there would be nothing in this material to contradict her. Who's to say if there was a Bible in her room? Who's to say if she was reading "The Strand"? *(John takes Halbrech's clipboard and reads.)*
JOHN. "Take me up. Take me up. Take me all the way to the Hebrides."
HALBRECH. "There are others."
JOHN. She says she's Welsh. Why the Hebrides?
HALBRECH. She doesn't remember those first words she spoke last night ... after she said "ice."
JOHN. "There are others." There are no more living survivors. The last died a year ago. A baby that night. *(Pause. John gets an idea, goes into gear.)* I'll need to take some photographs, we have cameras, yes?
HALBRECH. Yes.
JOHN. *(He starts gathering up books. He seems to be searching for specific things on selected pages in the books.)* We'll need film developed this afternoon if I'm going to do what I want. *Bribe* them if they say it'll take longer.
HALBRECH. What are we going to do?

25

JOHN. *(Intent on his work.)* Me to know. You to butt out.

HALBRECH. Are *all* the Astors as *involved* with the Titanic as you?

JOHN. I wouldn't know. *(John closes the last book. He pops a stack into Halbrech's arms.)* Run along. We're going to the movies. *(Blackout. End of scene.)*

Scene 2

John and the Woman, she in her bathrobe again. A slide projector is set-up on the end table, its lens focused out front. John holds a remote control switch in his hand.

JOHN. You know what a nickelodeon is? A lantern show?

WOMAN. *(Nods.)* Have them in Llechryd.

JOHN. *(Smiles.)* Yes, all the really *big* towns. Well, they've advanced a good deal since you might have seen them last. Photographs are not unknown of course. Moving pictures too, in 1912, although I'm not sure Georges Melies or Mack Sennett or D.W. Griffith have yet trundled Mr. Edison's invention all the way to Llechryd.

WOMAN. I have heard.

JOHN. Well, it's still a lantern show for *us* today. Should be fun. Pictures. Snap shots. Of faces. Of rooms. Of a ship. Forgive the quality. *(John presses the switch. Room lights dim, and a light streams out of the projector. John and the Woman face out front. John presses the switch again.)* Woman on the Promenade Deck. Know her?

WOMAN. *(Looks hard.)* I'm not sure. *(John presses switch.)*

JOHN. Family on the Boat Deck. Look familiar?

WOMAN. *(Squints.)* Could be. Not a very good picture.

JOHN. We do tend to think of that world in black and white, don't we? *(John presses switch.)* Elderly gentleman?

WOMAN. *(Shakes head.)* No. *(John presses switch.)*

JOHN. Little boy?

WOMAN. *(Matter of fact.)* No. *(John presses switch.)*

JOHN. Musician?

WOMAN.   *(Matter of fact.)* No. *(John presses switch.)*

JOHN.   Children in the nursery? *(Pause.)*

WOMAN.   *(A long gaze out front.)* Wait. Wait. *(She looks at John, almost giggles.)* No. *(John fumes. He presses switch.)*

JOHN.   Couple at the gangway.

WOMAN.   *(Bored.)* No. *(John presses switch.)*

JOHN.   Lady with a funny hat.

WOMAN.   *(Snickers.)* No. *(John presses switch.)*

JOHN.   Black steward.

WOMAN.   *(Obviously a fake photo.)* No. *(John looks at Woman.)*

JOHN.   All right. Now, let's take a different perspective. *(John presses switch.)*

WOMAN.   *(Starts.)* What is that?

JOHN.   That is under the sea. These next photographs are of a ship found at the bottom of the Atlantic a few years ago. *(John presses switch.)* The prow of the ship. *(John presses switch.)* A barnacle-encrusted railing. *(John presses switch.)* The Captain's wheel. *(John presses switch.)* Porthole. *(John presses switch.)* Disembodied head. *(The Woman gasps. Calmly.)* Oh, it's not a skull. It's a doll's head. Probably from the nursery. Still a smile on its lips. There are no bodies there. The bodies decomposed within a few years. By the early 1920s there couldn't have been a trace. Sorry. *(John presses switch. Slide changes.)* A pair of lady's high-button shoes — empty — lying on the bottom of the ocean floor. Only shoes and boots seem to have survived. Look at those, side by side. *(John presses switch.)* Chandelier from the Palm Court. *(John presses switch.)* Champagne bottle. *(John presses switch.)* Chamber pot. *(John presses switch.)* Deck chair. *(John presses switch.)* Titanic.

WOMAN.   It isn't.

JOHN.   Yes, it is.

WOMAN.   No, it isn't.

JOHN.   No, really, it is.

WOMAN.   *It isn't. (Pause.)*

JOHN.   Yes, you're right.

WOMAN.   Thank you. I just *saw* it a few *days* ago.

JOHN.   My mistake. Other ships do sink of course. Know ... *(John presses switch and moves D.)* ... him?

27

WOMAN. *(Shakes head.)* He looks very ... noble. Who *is* he? *(John stares at the photograph.)*
JOHN. I doubt you would have met. *(John presses switch, moves back U. Slide changes. Woman's eyes widen.)* That — some say — is the one. The iceberg. It was sighted by the German liner Prinz Adalbert on the morning of April 15, eleven hours after the sinking. A passenger onboard the Adalbert took this picture. *(John kneels next to her.)* Some say there was a red line, a red slash — like red paint — across the bottom of the iceberg. *(Points.)* Here. Unfortunately the photograph is in black and white. So we'll never really know. *(Still kneeling, John presses switch.)* Unidentified man at the third class staircase.
WOMAN. *(Automatically.)* Astor.
JOHN. I'm sorry?
WOMAN. *(As if it's a foreign word.)* As-tor.
JOHN. *(Glancing at the picture, then at the Woman.)* That's an unidentified man at the third class staircase. He's not an Astor. *(The Woman's eyes fill with tears.)* What. What is it? *(The Woman stares at the picture for a long moment, then begins to sob quietly. John slowly rises. He looks at her for another moment, then turns again to look out front at the slide. A long pause. The Woman raises her head to face John. John returns her gaze.)*
WOMAN. I just wanted to go on. I just wanted to go on. I just wanted to go to the household of Mrs. George Haverland Coe of Pittsburgh, Pennsylvania. *(The Woman continues to look at John. John looks back out front. Blackout. End of scene.)*

Scene 3

John alone. Lights are low. The projector beams out front. John stands off to the side, staring out front. A moment. The outer door opens and Halbrech — in her raincoat, with her briefcase — comes in quickly. She shuts the door behind her. She seems flushed and eager.

JOHN. *(Still staring front.)* You're late.
HALBRECH. *(Smiles.)* I have news.

JOHN. You're late, where were you?

HALBRECH. *(Takes coat off, smiling.)* Things to do, places to go, people to see. Did she identify any of the photos?

JOHN. Not directly. But her temperature certainly went up a few degrees on this. *(John indicates whatever is projected on the fourth wall.)*

HALBRECH. *(Squints.)* What is it?

JOHN. Unidentified man at the third class staircase.

HALBRECH. Who is he?

JOHN. *(Balefully.)* I don't know. That's why we call him "unidentified." *(Beat.)*

HALBRECH. Did she *say* anything? *Identify* him? *Name* him? *(Beat.)*

JOHN. *(Looks away.)* No.

HALBRECH. *(Looking out front.)* Then what are we supposed to see? He's just a man ... unlucky enough to be on the Titanic. *(John looks at the picture.)*

JOHN. I used to have a dream ... where I'm standing at the docks at Southampton, April 10, 1912, the day the Titanic left on its voyage. I'm standing in the crowd below the gangplank, and ... I cannot find my ticket. *I know I belong onboard. I know I have a place.* They *have* to let me onboard. Because I'm the only one who knows what's going to happen. And then I look up and I see that the ship has begun to slide from the dock, and the crowds have stopped cheering and the faces have vanished and the ship has disappeared and I am surrounded by darkness. I am alone on the edge of the sea.

HALBRECH. *(Watching him carefully.)* And you want to board the ship so you can *warn* them? *(Beat.)*

JOHN. I want to board the ship ... so I can *be there* when it comes. *(Beat. John turns off projector.)* Never mind. You're right. He's just a man unlucky enough to be on the Titanic.

HALBRECH. *(Tentatively.)* Did she identify Titanic *as* Titanic?

JOHN. No confusions. No mistaking it for the Lusitania or the Andrea Doria or the Queen Mary.

HALBRECH. What did she say about the Hebrides?

JOHN. Nothing.

HALBRECH. You asked her about the Hebrides and she said

nothing?

JOHN. I didn't ask her about the Hebrides.

HALBRECH. And "Take me up"?

JOHN. I didn't ask her about "Take me up."

HALBRECH. "There are others"?

JOHN. She seemed tired.

HALBRECH. Well. There *are* others. *(Halbrech smiles. John looks at her. Halbrech takes a yellowed newsclipping from her brief-case.)* Clipping. Last year. "Last Survivor of the Titanic Dies." Stamford, England. A Mr. A.L. Richardson, age three at the time of the disaster. You took that "Last" for granted. *(Halbrech hands another piece of paper to John.) This* one. Miss Frances Kittle. Number Two Cape Race, Ogunquit, Maine. Listed "F. Kittle," a survivor on the Carpathia's manifest, April 15, 1912. Her name disappears off the survivor lists in 1966. But she didn't die. She just stopped responding to inquiries. She's alive. Living at Number Two Cape Race, Ogunquit. Sixty miles from here. I talked to her. I *told* her. *(John stands.)*

JOHN. This is a breach — Our *agreement* — !

HALBRECH. She said she wanted to come here. She's frail, she's in a wheelchair. She has a nurse with her at all times. She wouldn't see me at first. And then she did. I showed her everything we had. She very much wants to see ... Winifred. *(John stares at Halbrech. Silence.)*

JOHN. When does she come? *(Halbrech smiles triumphantly.)*

HALBRECH. *Now. (Blackout. End of scene.)*

Scene 4

Halbrech and the Woman, she in her white robe.

HALBRECH. This is not meant to harm you. This is not meant to frighten you. She is very old. She simply wants to meet you.

WOMAN. And you want me to meet her. *(Halbrech nods. Pause.)*

30

HALBRECH.   What Mr. Astor has been doing with you —
bringing you here, keeping you here — would be completely
unacceptable in my profession, would be unheard of, would
be a crime. *(Beat.)*   Of course it *worked.* In my profession, I
work with those who *can* speak ... but *won't* speak. It often
takes months, *years* to get someone to ... *break* that kind of
silence.
WOMAN.   Is it lonely to spend time in such silence?
HALBRECH.   *(Deadpan.)* I live in Iceland, what's the difference.
     The thing is sometimes ... as much as I *want* them to ...
when they speak ... it's such a disappointment. Their words and
thoughts are always so much *smaller* than the ones I've made
up for them in their silence. *(Halbrech looks back at the Woman.)*
Until now.
     She won't hurt you. She just wants to ... speak with you.
WOMAN.   I trust you. You're my doctor. *(Pause.)*
HALBRECH.   I should tell you. I'm not a doctor. Not in the
way you mean. I *am* a professional, my superiors at the hospital give me a good deal of responsibility; I had *some* medical
school training a couple of lives ago, before I got dropped out,
got married, got divorced, ran away to that godforsaken place
in the middle of the Atlantic. I *will* have my doctorate *soon*
though. "All but the dissertation." *(Beat.)* None of this makes
much sense to you, does it?
WOMAN.   *(Simply.)* Yes. You're not what you seem.
HALBRECH.   *(Nods.)* We'll want you to wear this again.
(Halbrech holds up the dress and shawl. The Woman takes them.) I
want you to know: I believe ... *(The Woman looks at Halbrech.
Halbrech stops herself, changes gear.)* I believe you'll do very well.
(Beat.)
WOMAN   When does she come?
HALBRECH.   Now. *(Blackout. End of scene.)*

Scene 5

John and Miss Kittle.

Miss Kittle is a handsome woman, tall, regal, straight-backed with a strong face. Very old. Dressed in black — lace, shawl, high Victorian collar. She sits in a wheelchair, her legs covered by a blanket.

John appears tense and nervous throughout.

JOHN.   It was when I saw Telly Savalas fingering my great grandmother's earrings ... I knew then I had to dedicate myself to *preserving* the Titanic's sacred memory. The whole televised exhibition was violent in its disrespect. I stood transfixed before a television set. That bald man posturing there, somewhere in France, as so-called "experts" in rented tuxedos and clip-on ties sat upon a stage under a tacky chandelier and smeared their fingers over the coins, the money-boxes, the silverware, the jewelry ... all *ripped* from the cold, peaceful corpses' fingers. *(Beat.)*

MISS KITTLE.   *(Deadpan.)* There weren't actually *corpses*, were there?

JOHN.   Pardon-me?

MISS KITTLE.   There weren't actually *corpses*, they didn't actually find *corpses*, there weren't really the remains of *corpses*? *(Beat.)*

JOHN.   I was ... speaking metaphorically.

MISS KITTLE.   Yes, of course you were, dear. Will she be coming out soon?

JOHN.   Yes! Dr. Halbrech just wants to makes sure she's ready. Do you need anything?

MISS KITTLE.   If I do, you can get my nurse on the other side of that door. Is it ... *stuffy* in here?

JOHN.   We ... keep the temperature fairly *high*. I *should* tell you: in this place there are certain *words* we don't use in front of her.

MISS KITTLE. Words?

JOHN. Like ... "air-conditioner." Words a woman from 1912 couldn't possibly have known. Trip-her-up sort of thing. We've managed to be pristine on this point. I'm sure you'll follow our lead.

MISS KITTLE. When Dr. Halbrech told me about the situation, I expected a very different ... place. I expected a hospital. Or a sanitarium. A converted mansion, or one of those ghastly glass and steel things. But *this* ... from the outside this looks so much ... so much like a ...

JOHN. Gas station.

MISS KITTLE. Yes.

JOHN. That's what it was. The cinderblock and the tank holes out front give it away. Abandoned years ago. It's perfect for this. Isolated, nothing around for miles, just the coast road and the sea. Room enough inside to build this room and her bedroom, connect the plumbing and pipes, space on the other side of this wall for monitors, a hot plate, a cot. *Heating* works rather well, don't you think? All done in less than a week.

MISS KITTLE. And you decided this was preferable to a hospital.

JOHN. Oh, she's perfectly taken care of here. Dr. Halbrech is a specialist in this area.

MISS KITTLE. *(Deadpan.)* Dr. Halbrech specializes in passengers of the Titanic?

JOHN. She's not being held against her will, she can leave anytime she likes. All she has to do is ... *say.*

MISS KITTLE. And she hasn't?

JOHN. No. She hasn't.

MISS KITTLE. Do you expect me to recognize her?

JOHN. No, not at all, after eighty years, hardly. *She*, on the other hand, may *think* you *can.*

MISS KITTLE. Why?

JOHN. Well, you're *authentic. She's* ... *(Uneasy pause. John takes paper from pocket.)* I, uh, I've prepared a list of questions for you to pose her. Specifics about ... the night. I thought there might be some details you might not ... that you might have-

MISS KITTLE. Forgotten?

JOHN. Well ... if you find yourself at a loss, I'll be right there. *(He pockets the list.)* I'm ... I'm surprised more people don't try to seek you out. The "last living survivor of the Titanic." It's ... quite a ... *thrill. (Laughs nervously.)*

MISS KITTLE. There was a time when it wouldn't have been so strange to meet one. There were 705 of us. You just had to go to the right parties.

JOHN. But *you've* always lived in Maine, on the coast, in ... seclusion.

MISS KITTLE. For eighty years.

JOHN. Never married?

MISS KITTLE. *(Deadpan.)* Not *so far.* I understand from Dr. Halbrech that you know quite a lot about the Titanic.

JOHN. I do, yes.

MISS KITTLE. Why? Other ships have been lost, after all. All the time.

JOHN. *(Increasingly agitated.)* The Titanic was different. The Titanic was the greatest ocean liner ever built, carrying aboard it the most glittering figures of its day. The Titanic represented the bounds of modern society, for its achievements, for its glory, for its pride, for its arrogance — for a civilization creating a structure which could not help but drag its creators down to their deaths. The Titanic was a metaphor! *(Beat.)*

MISS KITTLE. *(Wry.)* Of course, we didn't think of it that way at the *time.*

JOHN. But ... but the *stories!* Philadelphia millionaires playing bridge in the smoking lounge right through the end. Benjamin Guggenheim dressing in full evening clothes and opera cape. And my own great grandfather, John Jacob Astor, standing on the promenade deck with his faithful valet at his side as the ship plunged beneath the waves.

MISS KITTLE. *(Deadpan.)* Halcyon Days.

JOHN. Of course. there was great *shame* as well. The SS Californian that sat ten miles away and didn't lift a finger. The wireless operators who didn't send up the ice warnings fast enough. And, of course, the myth of the man who got off the ship dressed as a woman. At any rate, anything you can do that will make her ... *uncomfortable* ... make her *squirm* ... well, that would be quite the thing.

MISS KITTLE. *(Staring at John.)* Oh, I enjoy watching people squirm.

JOHN. I should warn you: the woman ... cries on occasion. Part of the performance, don't be alarmed. She cries at photographs of the real victims. A shoddy approximation of survivor guilt.

MISS KITTLE. What?

JOHN. Survivor guilt. It's common to ... well ... you would know better than I.

MISS KITTLE. Why?

JOHN. *(Nervously.)* Well ... you're the last living survivor of the Titanic.

MISS KITTLE. *(A nod to the bedroom.)* Maybe *not.* I've never understood "survivor guilt." I lived, they died. Who's to say who's better off? One always makes a bargain to pay for the grace of God. But only if you can transform yourself. And whatever you transform yourself into, you must remain so forever. You define your future in the greatest moment of terror you have ever known. That which kept you alive ... will be what you are for the rest of your life. *(Pause.)*

JOHN. Miss Kittle?

MISS KITTLE. Yes?

JOHN. Do you *dream* about the Titanic? *(Beat.)*

MISS KITTLE. No.

JOHN. Never?

MISS KITTLE. Mr. Astor, when I was picked up by the Carpathia the day after the sinking ... I did not speak a word to a single soul. Not for days, not for weeks, not for months. And when we reached America, I returned to my family's home, went inside, closed the door, and I have not set foot outside its walls ... until today. I don't *have* to *dream* about the Titanic. A dream is a name we give our thoughts. *(Beat.)* Do *you* dream, Mr. Astor? Of the Titanic?

JOHN. Yes.

MISS KITTLE. Do you dream you're on the Titanic? *(Pause.)*

JOHN. *(Almost sad.)* No. No, I don't dream I'm *on* the Titanic.

MISS KITTLE.   But if you *had* been on the Titanic ... what do you think you would have done?

JOHN.   Behaved like a gentleman. Stood on the promenade deck, in the clear cold night ... stood there in full evening clothes, as the ship slid beneath the waves.

MISS KITTLE.   Alone? Why would anyone want to die alone? *(John looks at Miss Kittle.)* You're a very strange man, Mr. Astor. You're nostalgic for a disaster you never knew.

JOHN.   We should start. *(John moves to the bedroom door.)*

MISS KITTLE.   Mr. Astor: Don't be taken in by your dreams. There was more to the Titanic than the myth would have you believe. What you see, Mr. Astor, is just the tip. *(John opens the bedroom door. Halbrech and the Woman, again in her dress and shawl, enter. John closes the door behind them. The Woman looks at Miss Kittle. Pause.)*

Let's start with a joke. Do you know what the cast said when they heard the promiscuous actress had gone down on the Titanic? "Not bloody surprising." *(The Woman blinks, looks at Halbrech and John. Then they all turn to look at Miss Kittle, dumbfounded.)*

Come closer, my dear. Closer. Turn around. Turn around, dear. *(The Woman does so.)* Yes. My, my, yes. The years have certainly been kinder to you than they have to me. I understand you and I are part of a rather exclusive club. Sit. *(The Woman sits.)*

This is a horrid little room, isn't it? Simply ghastly. You do want to leave it, don't you? Just say so, dear, and they'll have to let you go. Otherwise, you're being held against your will. All you have to do is *say. (The Woman looks at John and Halbrech. Finally, she settles back in the deck chair, comfortably. Miss Kittle smiles admiringly.)*

Very good. You're supposed to believe I can recognize you, out of a thousand dead faces from a single night almost a century ago. "Oh, yes," I'll say, "she was the pretty one I saw playing with those chunks of ice on A-Deck." Or: "Impossible! I memorized them all, and this one is not one of them!" *Nonsense.* Mr. Astor has compiled a list of questions for me to ask you. In case I've forgotten. Mr. Astor knows everything about the Titanic. Mr. Astor is a romantic. And a romantic knows all good things — in the end — must die. A fishing boat found you on an iceberg, dressed as a young woman would have dressed that night. I have been told what you have said, that nothing you have said contradicts the known facts. You have spoken. Well. Let's speak some more. I have a list of questions ... *(John takes out his list and stands next to Miss Kittle. She looks up at him with withering scorn.)* ... which *I* have prepared. *(John looks at Halbrech, replaces his list, moves to the rear.)* Are you ready, my dear? *(The Woman looks at Halbrech, who smiles, nods. The Woman looks back to Miss Kittle, nods.)* Good. First class passengers were separated from second and third class passengers by a gate at the top of a staircase. What was the gate made of? *(Beat.)*

WOMAN.   Wood. But the locks were made of steel.

MISS KITTLE.   Correct. Men and women below decks in steerage had to follow certain rules those of us above did not. What did third class men and women have to do?

WOMAN.   The men slept on one side of steerage ... and the women on the other.

MISS KITTLE.   Correct. A *pity*, but correct. The lifeboat drill had gone smoothly enough earlier in the voyage. On what day at sea was the Titanic's lifeboat drill? *(Pause.)*

WOMAN.   There *was* no lifeboat drill on the Titanic. *(Miss Kittle smiles and chuckles admiringly.)*

MISS KITTLE.   Quite right. You were apparently a third class passenger. Third class passengers could only come above their quarters to First Class for *one reason*. What was it?

WOMAN.   Services. On Sunday.

MISS KITTLE.   Correct. And where did third class passengers have to sit for those services?

WOMAN.   At the rear.

MISS KITTLE.   Correct.

WOMAN.   Except.... *(Beat.)*

MISS KITTLE.   "Except"?

WOMAN.   *(Staring at Miss Kittle.)* Except ... for me.

MISS KITTLE. Oh, *really?* And why is that? Go on.

WOMAN. *(Putting a memory together.)* I was late. Coming to the service. There were no seats left by the time I came up, so ... *(Pause.)*

MISS KITTLE. Go on, my dear.

WOMAN. So I sat in the front.

MISS KITTLE. How very daring.

WOMAN. In the fourth row. *(Beat.)*

MISS KITTLE. Yes.

WOMAN. It was crowded. A man.... A man. A man ... gave up his seat for me. *(Pause.)*

MISS KITTLE. *(Staring back.)* He ... gave up his seat.

WOMAN. I was as close to him ... as I am to you. *(Pause.)*

MISS KITTLE. *(Tight.)* Take me out of here.

JOHN. *(Confused.)* Excuse-me?

MISS KITTLE. Take me out of here! You're all very clever, but I will not be part of a stunt concocted by three people for heaven only knows what end!

JOHN. Miss Kittle —

HALBRECH. We haven't concocted any —

MISS KITTLE. There *were* no *third class passengers* allowed to attend the first class services.

JOHN. *(Glancing back and forth.)* No thir —?

MISS KITTLE. This woman was never on the Titanic! Look at her! There is no depth to that face, there is no darkness in those eyes. There is no horror, there is no awe, there is no loss! I have never laid eyes on this woman and she has never laid eyes on me. *(To all of them.)* You're a cheap carnival act. *(She wheels herself to face the outside door.)* Take me from this place. *(The Woman looks up.)*

WOMAN. *(Simply.)* You're right. *(Miss Kittle wheels herself back around to face the Woman.)* This lady never laid eyes on me. And I never laid eyes on this lady. This lady and I were not on the Titanic together.

MISS KITTLE. *(A smile.)* Thank you, dear. *(She wheels away again.)*

WOMAN. When I laid eyes on this lady, she was not a lady.

She had short hair, a small mustache, a burly frame, and how she managed to fit into the dress and the shawl only God can say. *(Miss Kittle swerves her wheelchair around to face the Woman. Quick blackout. End of scene.)*

Scene 6

John alone. He holds a small piece of paper in front of him. For the first time, his tie is loosened.

JOHN. *(Reading from paper.)* "The sudden death of Miss Frances Kittle ..." "... of *Mr.* Francis Kittle ..." "... of the *person* Kittle ..." *(The outer door opens. Halbrech, in her raincoat, enters. She shuts the door behind her. Not at all sure of himself.)* I was preparing a statement. For the authorities. Police.

HALBRECH. *(Brisk, tight, on edge.)* Kaspar and Dane put the body in the van. I'm going to the hospital, one of us has to stay with ... *her.* Give me the keys to your car.

JOHN. The keys?

HALBRECH. There's no room in the van for me. Kaspar, Dane, the nurse, Miss ... Kittle's body. Give me your keys.

JOHN. You *have* to go?

HALBRECH. Unless *you* want to answer questions. *(Beat. John plops his keys into her hand. A glance at the bedroom door.)* Keep her locked-up.

JOHN. *(Moves to Halbrech.)* What if, what if she asks to go? I'll have to let her go if she asks to go.

HALBRECH. *(Steel.)* Keep her locked up. *(Halbrech glances at the bedroom door.)* There's something else. A Canadian oil ship picked-up a man off the coast of Nova Scotia this afternoon. An elderly man in a kind of naval uniform. White beard. Bullhorn in his hand. Captain's braid on his cap. He was sitting on a slab of ice. He says his name is "Smith." Captain of the RMS Titanic out of Liverpool. *(Pause.)*

JOHN. This is a tabloid story ...

HALBRECH. I heard it on the radio.

JOHN.   Serious?

HALBRECH.   *(Deadpan.) Public* radio. He's being taken to Halifax for observation. Keep her locked-up. We'll be back in a few hours. *(Beat.)* There *are* others. *(Halbrech exits. John stares at the bedroom door. Blackout. End of scene.)*

Scene 7

John alone again, tense, sitting in the deck chair, the lights low. After a moment, there is a click. John turns to the bedroom door. The doorknob turns. John reacts. The door slowly swings open. The Woman enters behind John. She is in her dress, her hair down now. She closes the door behind her. Click. John stands up, turns. They face each other.

WOMAN.   We're alone. We've never been alone before. Without them watching.

JOHN.   *(A catch.)* The, uh, others will be back soon. *(Beat.)*

WOMAN.   You're afraid of me. Aren't you? *(Pause.)*

JOHN.   *(Swallows.)* I, uh, I think we've had enough of this. I want your confession. *Now.* In writing. I don't care if you're Finnish, Swedish, Russian, Norwegian, or two weeks out of Pittsburgh, Pennsylvania singing "Nearer My God to Thee"! *(John slams down a piece of paper and a pen.)* There! *Now!* *(Tense face-off.)* I *mean* it! *(Pause.)*

WOMAN.   *(Smiles wickedly.)* You're *verrrrry* afraid of me. You get things wrong. You know that, don't you?

JOHN.   "Wrong"?

WOMAN.   *(Nods.)* The band never played "Nearer My God to Thee". They played ragtime and palm court music and one Episcopal hymn called "Autumn." "Nearer My God to Thee" would have been nice, too.

JOHN.   *(A certain "British spine.")* An Episcopal hymn, I should think, would be terribly difficult to identify so far beneath the promenade deck in steerage. Especially for a Welsh Methodist.

WOMAN.   We always know the songs that are sung by our betters. *(Beat.)*

JOHN. *(A gamble, a dare.)* Sing. *Sing it. (Pause. John and the Woman are in a face-off. Finally, the Woman looks away and moves from him. John smiles. Becoming cocky again.)* What's the matter! Called your *bluff? I know you!* Better than you know yourself! You're *pathetic! (The Woman turns to John.)*

WOMAN. You very much want to kiss me, don't you.

JOHN. *(Shaken.) What? Please.* But I forget: you've been without someone for such a very long time, all those years floating about on the ice you must be cold as death!

WOMAN. Does that excite you?

JOHN. *(A tremble in his voice.)* I don't have to stay in this room with you. I can leave you alone and wait outside. Watch you from outside.

WOMAN. I know you watch me. You want to hold my hand then? A gentleman would hold a lady's hand before he kisses her.

JOHN. *I do not want to kiss you! (Beat.)*

WOMAN. *(Saucy.)* P'raps you're *not* a gentleman. *(Shrugs.)* All right. *(The Woman starts to move towards her bedroom.)*

JOHN. *(Takes step.)* Wait! *(The Woman stops, turns.)*

WOMAN. Do you want to follow me? *(Pause. John moves a step. Stops. Steps back. Fixing her eyes on him.)* What if you whispered it to me? I wouldn't tell a soul. It would be just you ... and me. I'm someone you *could* share this with. I'm a kindred spirit. I want to help. *Speaking* will help. *(Beat.)*

JOHN. *(Blurts.)* They found the captain!

WOMAN. They'll find more. *(Beat.)* Until you know what you must do. The next one will be found twenty-five minutes from now. A man. In black silk evening clothes, wearing a white life jacket. He will be found in the Badlands of South Dakota. He will say his name is John Jacob Astor. He will be asked if it is true that he saw his wife to safety and then calmly stood on the Promenade Deck to wait for his fate, and he will say: "The sons of bitches kept me from the boats, and when I get back to New York I'm gonna sue the bastards for every penny they've got!"

JOHN. He would *never* say that!

WOMAN. *He'll say that.*

41

JOHN.   He was a *gentleman!* The Astors are gentlemen! *I* am a gentleman!

WOMAN.   *Are* you? *(John starts. She smiles. John bolts for the outer door, tries it. No luck.)* It's locked. *(John looks at her in panic. He pounds on the door.)* They've gone. *(John digs into his pocket.)* You gave her your keys. Remember? *(John whirls on her.)*

JOHN.   *(Very intense.)* Listen to me! I understand why you would do this, this *performance*, this *act!* Ever since you were a child *nothing* has felt right, not friends, not family, not place, not time; you've always wondered if you were in the wrong place, you've always wondered if you were the wrong person. And then one day you see a, a *picture* — of a ship — a painting in rich oils, dark and shining, royal blue water and bright blue sky, a navy blue hull and red water line and the funnels, the smokestacks roaring a steam-white plumage into the night. And you think of the people who boarded the ship and how they defined themselves in that one night — at their best, at their finest — having the *chance* to prove in that one cold, bitter night just who they were, to find out just the sort of stuff they were *made* of! And suddenly you find you've come to the surface from deep down inside. You find your voice, and you don't recognize its richness or its accent, but it's *right*. And you stand in a certain way and you comb your hair in a certain way and you speak in a certain way, and it all *fits!* And who's to say it isn't *really* you because who were you really? I understand. Say that to me, and I'll understand. *(Pause. The Woman opens her mouth and begins to sing "Autumn" in a simple, clear voice.)*

WOMAN.

> "In the hour of pain and anguish,
> In the hour when death draws near,
> Suffer not our hearts to languish
> Suffer not our souls to fear.
>
> Let thy promise to be near us
> Fill our hearts with joy and peace,
> May thy presence sweetly cheer us,
> Till our conflicts all shall cease."

Who are you?

JOHN. *(About to break.)* I am John Jacob Ast —

WOMAN. No.

JOHN. I am —

WOMAN. No.

JOHN. I am — *(Pause. John collapses.) No.* I'm not. *(Beat.)*

WOMAN. Somewhere ... on the coast road ... the doctor is coming. She has been stopped in the village before returning. She has been told of a man in South Dakota who some years ago changed his name to John Jacob Astor. A quiet fellow, very smart, very clever, very lonely, with a penchant for acting like a man to the manor born. He has an obsession apparently. For a ship. A famous disaster. He disappeared the day a certain tabloid newspaper was delivered to his place of work — a place called a 7-Eleven. He's been missing three weeks now ... he and a great deal of money that doesn't belong to him. *(Beat.)* They're coming for you. Do you want to hold my hand *now?* *(John looks at her.)*

JOHN. Why are you here?

WOMAN. Because sometimes a voice can be heard, a cry can be heard ... across the desert, over the waves, deep into the sea. There's no place for you in this world. No one should be so alone. No one should die so alone. I didn't understand myself at first.... And then I heard that name ... and I saw that photograph ... and I began to remember ... remembering bit by bit, piece by piece ... until I remembered more than I ever knew. Everything ... everything except what happened that night.

JOHN. *Tell me.*

WOMAN. *(Afraid.)* I can't.

JOHN. Yes, you can. I am not an Astor, I have no great wealth, I am part of no great family. I came here to ... I wanted so to *believe* in you. I wanted so for you to be *real.* So I could *be there!* *(John kneels next to her.) Help me.* I'll help you. *Tell me. (Silence.)*

WOMAN. The first time I saw him was at the third class staircase. Sunday morning worship. Feeling the eyes across the room during the hymn and the admonition. And then the eyes meeting. A hat tipped. An offer of a walk along the deck on a Sunday afternoon. And then a spot of tea. And then supper. And more. And the questions. "What do you do before bed, darlin'?" "I read the Bible. And then — sometimes — my "Strand." But on Sunday, just the Bible." And you know how they keep us in third class. Men on one end, women on the other. Like we were children, and they who run the ship know better. But you can come from one end to the other. You can come down from high *above* as well. And it's dark out. And the sea and the sky and the stars have gone by. And indeed there is the Bible. Laid out on the blanket. Across my breast. Unopened. And the "Strand" even farther away. And the rap on the door then comes. And, yes, a talk would be lovely, although it's not really proper in the room. "Oh, I am going to work in the household of Mrs. George Haverland Coe of Pittsburgh, Pennsylvania. In-service just like yourself, but I could never claim a position as fancy as you. To be in service to such a fine family, I am very impressed indeed to be sure." And then more talk. And laughter, very hushed and silent. And then the question. And the question again. And again. And then an answer. And the Bible is placed aside near the "Strand." And then, in the dark, in the silence, in the murmur of the machines in the heart of the ship, a finger draws along the side ... and wakes. "It's the ghost of your aunt, Mrs. James, wagging a finger at her naughty niece." And I laugh. And we go on. And then there is another knock on the door. And voices in the passageway. "We should go up and see ..." "No, darlin', not yet." "We should go up and see what it is ..." "No, not yet. A little longer, darlin'. A little longer." But I want to see what it is, and I look out the porthole. And it is a sea of ice, mountains of ice going by, so beautiful in such a calm, black sea. We've stopped, and we can look out at this beautiful field of ice. "Let's go up," I say. "Let's go up and see." But we don't. "Listen to me, darlin'. I must go up to the master, or there'll be hell to pay. But I'll come back. You wait under the covers, and when I come back I'll take you up to see the ice. I know a way to get up to the first class Promenade Deck where we can see, and no one will know. I know a way up through a central passageway, a passageway that runs all the way through the length of the ship, from bow to stern. The officers call it "Park Lane." The crew calls it "Scotland Road." We'll go up, we'll go up all the way on "Scotland Road". And I'll show you the ice, I'll show you the mountains of ice. I'll take you up "Scotland Road." "Take me up. Take me up! *Take me all the way to the Hebrides!*" He was so beautiful. My handsome valet to the Astors. He never came back. *(She stares out front.)*

JOHN. *(Looking at her.)* A ... a *gentleman* ... would have come back. I would have come back. I would fight all the way down from the Promenade Deck through the crowds and the cries. I would come back ... for *you. (Pause. The Woman continues to stare out front. Finally:)*

WOMAN. *(Out front.)* Hold my hand.

JOHN. *(Looks at outer door.)* The doctor —

WOMAN. *(Out front.)* We shall be gone before she's here. And she will understand the silence.

JOHN. *(Kneels next to her.)* And the captain? And Colonel Astor? *(Sound: A low hum begins to well-up.)*

WOMAN. *(Out front.)* The captain is at his post, and Colonel Astor is with his wife in their stateroom.

JOHN. And the sea? And the stars?

WOMAN. *(Out front.)* They are beautiful. Can you see?

JOHN. *(Looks out, squints.)* It's a blank wall ...

WOMAN. *(Out front.)* No. *Look.*

JOHN. *(Looks.)* No. It *isn't* a blank wall. It's a *porthole. (They gaze out front like this, holding hands. A new sound is added to the low hum. The sound of the prow of the ship cutting evenly across the waves. The sounds build through to the end.)*

WOMAN. Yes.

JOHN. And I see the sky.

WOMAN. Yes.

JOHN. And the stars.

WOMAN. Yes.

JOHN. It's such a cold, *clear* night.

WOMAN. And the sea?

JOHN. And the sea is a black marble glass, like a mirror!

And we're gliding through the sea and the sky and the night, and I'm *here*, I'm really *here!*

WOMAN. *(Points out front.)* There. Do you see it?

JOHN. What?

WOMAN. *There!*

JOHN. What?

WOMAN. *(Closes her eyes.)* Look. *(A bright light begins to well-up on them.)*

JOHN. *(Staring wide-eyed.)* Yes. Yes, I *do* ... I see it ... It's *huge!* A huge, white mountain of ice! Getting closer! *Closer!* I can touch it! I can feel it! It's here! It's here! Hold my hand! Hold my hand! We'll go up, we'll go up, we'll go all the way up Scotland Road! *(Sound is roaring, lights a blast of white. John is staring out front, bracing for the collision.)* When does it come! *(The Woman's eyes open, flashing out front.)*

WOMAN. Now. *(Roaring sound sweeps up. Blistering lights — it looks as if John and the Woman might disappear into the blinding light. The lights dump out. The sound roars up even louder. Five second hold in the blackness. The black and white image of the iceberg wells-up again in the darkness. The roar rumbles on. There's a difference to the photograph of the iceberg now. At the bottom of the black and white photograph, across the bottom of the iceberg, is a red gash, a red slash, blood red. The image holds for a few seconds. The image slowly fades with the sound. Until it is darkness again. Until it is silent.)*

END OF PLAY

PROPERTY LIST

Paper (HALBRECH)
Clipboard (HALBRECH)
Elaborate dinner setting on silver tray:
    food
    crystal
    china
    silver
Wooden end table
Book (HALBRECH)
Ice bucket (JOHN)
Bottle of champagne (JOHN)
3 champagne flutes (JOHN)
Briefcase (HALBRECH)
Overnight bag (HALBRECH)
Watch (HALBRECH)
Key (HALBRECH)
Envelope (JOHN)
Mountain of books, magazines and papers (HALBRECH)
Small white T-shirt with writing (HALBRECH)
Slide projector with remote-control switch (JOHN)
Yellowed news clipping (HALBRECH)
Turn of the century dress and shawl
Piece of paper (JOHN)
Small piece of paper (JOHN)
Car keys (JOHN)
Paper and pen (JOHN)

SOUND EFFECTS

A large, powerful ocean liner moving through the sea:
    the hum of great turbines
    the low crushing of waves as the prow cuts through
        the water

TODAY'S HOTTEST NEW PLAYS

❏ **MOLLY SWEENEY by Brian Friel, Tony Award-Winning Author of** *Dancing at Lughnasa.* Told in the form of monologues by three related characters, *Molly Sweeney* is mellifluous, Irish storytelling at its dramatic best. Blind since birth, Molly recounts the effects of an eye operation that was intended to restore her sight but which has unexpected and tragic consequences. *"Brian Friel has been recognized as Ireland's greatest living playwright. Molly Sweeney confirms that Mr. Friel still writes like a dream. Rich with rapturous poetry and the music of rising and falling emotions...Rarely has Mr. Friel written with such intoxicating specificity about scents, colors and contours." - New York Times.* [2M, 1W]

❏ **SWINGING ON A STAR (The Johnny Burke Musical) by Michael Leeds. 1996 Tony Award Nominee for Best Musical.** The fabulous songs of Johnny Burke are perfectly represented here in a series of scenes jumping from a 1920s Chicago speakeasy to a World War II USO Show and on through the romantic high jinks of the Bob Hope/Bing Crosby "Road Movies." Musical numbers include such favorites as "Pennies from Heaven," "Misty," "Ain't It a Shame About Mame," "Like Someone in Love," and, of course, the Academy Award winning title song, "Swinging on a Star." *"A WINNER. YOU'LL HAVE A BALL!" - New York Post. "A dazzling, toe-tapping, finger-snapping delight!" - ABC Radio Network. "Johnny Burke wrote his songs with moonbeams!" - New York Times.* [3M, 4W]

❏ **THE MONOGAMIST by Christopher Kyle.** Infidelity and mid-life anxiety force a forty-something poet to reevaluate his 60s values in a late 80s world. *"THE BEST COMEDY OF THE SEASON. Trenchant, dark and jagged. Newcomer Christopher Kyle is a playwright whose social satire comes with a nasty, ripping edge - Molière by way of Joe Orton." - Variety. "By far the most stimulating playwright I've encountered in many a buffaloed moon." - New York Magazine. "Smart, funny, articulate and wisely touched with rue...the script radiates a bright, bold energy." - The Village Voice.* [2M, 3W]

❏ **DURANG/DURANG by Christopher Durang.** These cutting parodies of *The Glass Menagerie* and *A Lie of the Mind,* along with the other short plays in the collection, prove once and for all that Christopher Durang is our theater's unequivocal master of outrageous comedy. *"The fine art of parody has returned to theater in a production you can sink your teeth and mind into, while also laughing like an idiot." - New York Times. "If you need a break from serious drama, the place to go is Christopher Durang's silly, funny, over-the-top sketches." - TheatreWeek.* [3M, 4W, flexible casting]

DRAMATISTS PLAY SERVICE, INC.
440 Park Avenue South, New York, New York 10016 212-683-8960 Fax 212-213-1539

TODAY'S HOTTEST NEW PLAYS

❏ **THREE VIEWINGS by Jeffrey Hatcher.** Three comic-dramatic monologues, set in a midwestern funeral parlor, interweave as they explore the ways we grieve, remember, and move on. *"Finally, what we have been waiting for: a new, true, idiosyncratic voice in the theater. And don't tell me you hate monologues; you can't hate them more than I do. But these are much more: windows into the deep of each speaker's fascinating, paradoxical, unique soul, and windows out into a gallery of surrounding people, into hilarious and horrific coincidences and conjunctions, into the whole dirty but irresistible business of living in this damnable but spellbinding place we presume to call the world."* - New York Magazine. [1M, 2W]

❏ **HAVING OUR SAY by Emily Mann.** The Delany Sisters' Bestselling Memoir is now one of Broadway's Best-Loved Plays! Having lived over one hundred years apiece, Bessie and Sadie Delany have plenty to say, and their story is not simply African-American history or women's history...it is our history as a nation. *"The most provocative and entertaining family play to reach Broadway in a long time."* - New York Times. *"Fascinating, marvelous, moving and forceful."* - Associated Press. [2W]

❏ **THE YOUNG MAN FROM ATLANTA Winner of the 1995 Pulitzer Prize. by Horton Foote.** An older couple attempts to recover from the suicide death of their only son, but the menacing truth of why he died, and what a certain Young Man from Atlanta had to do with it, keeps them from the peace they so desperately need. *"Foote ladles on character and period nuances with a density unparalleled in any living playwright."* - NY Newsday. [5M, 4W]

❏ **SIMPATICO by Sam Shepard.** Years ago, two men organized a horse racing scam. Now, years later, the plot backfires against the ringleader when his partner decides to come out of hiding. *"Mr. Shepard writing at his distinctive, savage best."* - New York Times. [3M, 3W]

❏ **MOONLIGHT by Harold Pinter.** The love-hate relationship between a dying man and his family is the subject of Harold Pinter's first full-length play since *Betrayal*. *"Pinter works the language as a master pianist works the keyboard."* - New York Post. [4M, 2W, 1G]

❏ **SYLVIA by A.R. Gurney.** This romantic comedy, the funniest to come along in years, tells the story of a twenty-two year old marriage on the rocks, and of Sylvia, the dog who turns it all around. *"A delicious and dizzy new comedy."* - New York Times. *"FETCHING! I hope it runs longer than Cats!"* - New York Daily News. [2M, 2W]

DRAMATISTS PLAY SERVICE, INC.
440 Park Avenue South, New York, New York 10016 212-683-8960 Fax 212-213-1539